START UP DREAMS

Sai Kiran Sekharamahanti

BLUEROSE PUBLISHERS
India | U.K.

Copyright © Sekharamahanti 2024

All rights reserved by author. No part of this publication may be reproduced, stored in a retrieval system or transmitted in any form or by any means, electronic, mechanical, photocopying, recording or otherwise, without the prior permission of the author. Although every precaution has been taken to verify the accuracy of the information contained herein, the publisher assumes no responsibility for any errors or omissions. No liability is assumed for damages that may result from the use of information contained within.

BlueRose Publishers takes no responsibility for any damages, losses, or liabilities that may arise from the use or misuse of the information, products, or services provided in this publication.

For permissions requests or inquiries regarding this publication, please contact:

BLUEROSE PUBLISHERS
www.BlueRoseONE.com
info@bluerosepublishers.com
+91 8882 898 898
+4407342408967

ISBN: 978-93-5989-465-2

First Edition: April 2024

Preface

In the realms of reality and entrepreneurship, I share a personal odyssey—a genuine account of my journey through the startup landscape. With a sincere desire to illuminate the path less discussed, I bring forth not just the echoes of triumph but the resounding lessons embedded in setbacks. This narrative is not a chronicle of successes but a candid reflection on failures and challenges encountered in the pursuit of entrepreneurial dreams. It is an offering to those who harbor aspirations of traversing the startup terrain —an unfiltered tale meant to resonate with your own experiences, providing insights, fortitude, and a deeper understanding of the ever-evolving landscape of startups.

Embarking on a nostalgic journey, this reflective exploration delves into the roots of entrepreneurship. From childhood experiments with makeshift aquariums to venturing into menswear stalls with minimal funds, the entrepreneurial spirit persisted. In adulthood, the pursuit of impactful app ideas led to the establishment of "aptap," focusing on standalone apartment solutions.

Challenges, including financial constraints, team dedication issues, and unexpected setbacks, underline the unpredictable nature of the entrepreneurial path.

Navigating mobile app development, strategic shifts from freelancing to an in-house team highlight adaptability.

The journey unfolds with the establishment of dedicated office space, financial stability, and exploration of diverse revenue streams.

Facing capital challenges, a friends-and-family round enables the beta version launch, emphasizing adaptability and evolution.

User feedback prompts a pivotal redesign, focusing on simplicity and adaptability in a startup setting. The release within the community unveils unexpected challenges, teaching lessons on kindness and resilience. Financial shortfalls, operational challenges, and the impact of the COVID-19 pandemic mark a turning point, underscoring adaptableness, resilience, and acceptance of uncertainties.

The inception of "QuikServ" during the pandemic exemplifies adaptability, addressing unemployment and home service demands. The venture's success, despite setbacks, reveals untapped potential in tier III cities. Inspired by former employees turned entrepreneurs, mentoring emerging startups underscores dedication to fostering entrepreneurship. The journey, filled with successes and failures, highlights the ever-evolving nature of startups.

My primary aim is to offer guidance and insights to aspiring entrepreneurs.

Having navigated the unpredictable terrain of starting and running a business, I understand the unforeseen challenges that often accompany such ventures.

The motivation behind sharing this journey stems from a deep-rooted belief that by sharing our stories, we empower others to embark on their entrepreneurial paths with a bit more clarity and confidence. Whether you're at the beginning of your journey or facing hurdles along the way, this book is crafted to provide you with valuable perspectives and practical scenarios that I've been through.

I want to assure you that this narrative is not about pointing fingers or dwelling on mistakes. The identities of individuals who played roles in my journey are intentionally kept confidential, respecting their privacy and ensuring a focus on the lessons learned rather than personal details.

As you delve into the pages ahead, I encourage you to embrace the challenges, celebrate the victories, and glean insights that resonate with your own entrepreneurial aspirations. Happy reading, and may your journey be as enlightening and transformative.

Prologue:
The Entrepreneur's Odyssey

In the vast expanse of entrepreneurship, where dreams collide with reality and innovation intertwines with challenges, this book finds its origin. It is a chronicle born not just from ink and paper but from the countless moments of inspiration, struggle, and triumph that define the entrepreneurial odyssey.

The journey into the world of startups is nothing short of an adventure – an exploration of uncharted territories fueled by passion, guided by principles, and marked by the indomitable spirit of those who dare to dream big. As an entrepreneur, I've navigated the dynamic landscape where bold ideas meet the crucible of execution. Through the highs of innovation and the lows of uncertainty, the principles discussed in these pages have been my compass, steering me through the complexities of building and scaling a startup.

In the chapters that follow, we delve into the core elements that form the heartbeat of successful startups: high standards, operational integration, and discipline. These principles are not just abstract concepts; they are the threads woven into the fabric of every startup's narrative. They are the silent architects behind the scenes, shaping cultures, forging strategies, and propelling ventures toward lasting success.

This book is not a prescription but a conversation—an intimate dialogue between the pages where experiences, insights, and lessons learned come together. It's a bridge connecting the aspiring entrepreneur with the seasoned visionary, offering a roadmap through the twists and turns of the entrepreneurial journey.

As we embark on this exploration, let these words be more than a guide; let them be a reservoir of wisdom for those venturing into the exhilarating world of startups. This is a prologue to stories of innovation, resilience, and the pursuit of dreams—a prologue to your entrepreneurial journey.

And amidst the tales of triumph, we acknowledge the lessons learned from failure, for in those moments lie invaluable insights, shaping our understanding and fortifying our resolve. So, turn the page, join the conversation, and let the odyssey, with all its highs and lows, begin.

Acknowledgement

This entrepreneurial endeavor has been shaped by the unwavering support and contributions of a remarkable circle of individuals, and I express my heartfelt gratitude to each one.

To my mentors and advisors, your guidance has been instrumental in navigating the complexities of entrepreneurship. Your insights have been a compass, steering me toward success.

To my dedicated team, your hard work and commitment have been the driving force behind the accomplishments we celebrate today. Our collective efforts have defined the spirit of our startup.

To my friends and family, thank you for being the pillars of support. Your encouragement and more meaningful.

To my parents, your love and sacrifices have been the bedrock upon which I've built my dreams. Your unwavering belief has been a constant inspiration.

To my mother, Prameela Devi, your spirit continues to guide me. This work is a tribute to your enduring influence, shaping the principles shared within these pages.

To my wife, whose unwavering support and understanding have been my anchor. Your presence has been a source of strength and comfort throughout this entrepreneurial odyssey.

To my daughter, **Yuktika Krishna**, your innocence and joy remind me of the greater with boundless determination.

To every reader joining me on this adventure, may the lessons shared within these pages igniteyour entrepreneurial spirit.

Contents

The Fish Tank Startup: Nurturing Dreams, One Fish at a Time" 1

"Festive Ventures:Navigating Capital Constraints with Determination" 7

"Corporate Crossroads: NavigatingBetween Career and EntrepreneurialDreams" 14

"Idea Genesis to Startup Reality: Navigating Challenges and Embracing Collaboration" 20

"Navigating the Entrepreneurial Odyssey: Mentorship, Networking, and Unseen Allies" 27

"From Concept toTeam: Navigating the Formation of a Startup Core" 33

"Navigating App Development: Choosing the Right Team for Startup Success" 38

"Launching Into the Unknown: Beta Versions, Challenges, and Strategic Pivots" 43

"Redesign Realities: Navigating User Feedback and Office Woes" 49

"Unexpected Turns: Lessons In App Development and Unforeseen Alliances" 54

"Navigating Challenges: The Rise and Fall of My Startup Journey" 59

"Equity and Pressure- The Dual Faces of Startup Financing" 66

"The Journey of 'QuikServ' and the Rise of a Purposeful Second Venture" 71

The Fish Tank Startup: Nurturing Dreams, One Fish at a Time"

Back in the early 1990s, the absence of today's pervasive technology allowed my youthful curiosity to bloom in the realm of household pets. The hours, unclaimed by the screens of smartphones and computers, beckoned for a fulfilling hobby. Thus, the journey of raising pets commenced a journey that encompassed a diverse array of companions – cats, dogs, rabbits, turtles, ducks, hens, parrots, pigeons, and more.

Around the tender age of 9 or 10, a new fascination captivated my imagination – fish tanks or aquariums. These aquatic marvels boasted not only vibrant fish but also intricate accessories, such as a device resembling a stones adorning the tank's bottom and vibrant green underwater plants swaying with the water's rhythm.

Eager to partake in this underwater symphony, I became the proud owner of an aquarium, driven by my enthusiasm for the myriad fish breeds awaiting my care. Almost every other day, my eager feet led me to the nearby aquarium store, a place that transcended the typical pet shop of that era. Delving into the intricacies of the trade, I explored different breeds – golden fishes, red cups, black gold, silver moles, red moles, black moles, fighters, and a seemingly endless list.

It didn't escape my notice that some fish in the aquarium shop were lean while others sported a more robust physique, complete with protruding bellies. Inquiring with the store owner revealed that the plump ones were likely to deliver fingerlings in a few days, adding a new dimension to my thoughts – a potential revenue model.

The entrepreneurial spark ignited when I envisioned purchasing a fish today and selling hundreds of fish reproduction. One fine day, I acquired a pregnant black mole fish on the brink of delivering, eagerly informing my parents of my venture. Predictably, my mom expressed her usual skepticism, while my dad, acknowledging my determination, assisted me in arranging a light on a transparent glass jar. For context, this jar was none other than a repurposed 1 kg Horlicks (a sweet malted milk hot drink powder) bottle, complete with a 0-volt bulb arranged with my dad's guidance.

As an aspiring entrepreneur, my initial endeavors involved waking up every 30 minutes during the night to check if the fish had delivered. Despite my best efforts, I failed to stay vigilant throughout the night. However, the next morning brought the exciting discovery of around 40 fingerlings in the jar, marking a significant achievement for a young enthusiast.

This marked the inception of a simple marketing model. In an era lacking sophisticated communication channels, I resorted to visiting nearby friends to share the news of my newfound venture, offering to sell the fingerlings for making purchases despite minimal advertising.

Having initially acquired the fish for Rs.5, I successfully sold close to 20 fingerlings, pricing them between Rs.1 and Rs.3 each. As demand increased, so did the price, demonstrating the fundamental principles of supply and demand.

The crucial lesson emerged as my friends, attracted by their initial purchase of fingerlings, made more revenues to the aquarium shops. They initially invested in small fish jars or tanks, each priced at around Rs.50, to raise fingerlings. Over time, they developed a profound interest in the hobby, subsequently investing in aquariums, various fish breeds, and additional accessories, amounting to thousands of rupees during the 90s.

Size, age, gender, status, or professions are inconsequential when embarking on a startup journey –

Conclusion & Learnings: "In my early entrepreneurial endeavors with fish tanks at the age of 10, I learned the power of observation and adaptation. Spotting an opportunity in the aquarium trade, I ventured into breeding fish, turning a simple hobby into a profitable business. This experience taught me the fundamentals of supply and demand, showcasing the potential of creating a market where none existed. The lesson of being resourceful, embracing unforeseen opportunities, and the value of word-of-mouth marketing laid the foundation for my future entrepreneurial endeavors."

"Success is not final, failure is not fatal: It is the courage to continue that counts." - Winston S. Churchill

"Festive Ventures: Navigating Capital Constraints with Determination"

In the relentless march of time, my entrepreneurial zeal, undeterred by the constraints of adolescence and financial limitations, continued to burn brightly. Within the intimate cocoon of my close-knit circle of friends, I found a like-minded individual—a kindred spirit equally ablaze with imagination and a thirst for business ventures. Our discussions, filled with dreams of launching local stores across diverse segments, echoed with promise. However, the cruel reality of limited capital cast a shadow over these modest business aspirations, reminding us that our financial foundation rested on my father's monthly earnings—the bedrock upon which our aspirations stood.

Amidst the persistent financial challenges, a spark of innovation ignited in our minds. What if we ventured into a seasonal business that demanded minimal setup? This ingenious idea emerged during the festive aura of Christmas and the ensuing holiday season, a time when individuals sought new attire to embrace the celebratory spirit. The plan was simple yet revolutionary: inaugurate a menswear stall in a bustling locale, seeking the necessary parental approval. The funds initially designated for my festive attire became the seed capital for this seasonal enterprise. While my parents were supportive, their financial contribution was constrained. Undeterred, we approached this venture with a spirit of trial and exploration, ready to navigate the unknown.

Our journey led us to local wholesale vendors, where we immersed ourselves in the intricacies of pricing for various outfits. Unveiling their suppliers proved to be a challenging quest, as these merchants guarded their sources with a level of secrecy usually reserved for closely held treasures. Persistence eventually paid off when a kind-hearted gentleman disclosed a small town approximately 60 km from our city as the sourcing hub. However, the logistics of reaching this town posed a formidable challenge, given a single highway with heavy truck traffic connecting Chennai and Kolkata. Fearing our parents' apprehensions about the arduous journey, we chose to keep them in the dark about our ambitious plans.

This journey marked my first significant venture, a bold step taken with a resolute purpose. In an era devoid of smartphones and maps, our navigation relied on stopping at Dhabas and villages to confirm our route. Upon reaching our destination, a few wholesale dealers graciously received us, sourcing stock directly from factories. A senior distributor, moved by our entrepreneurial narrative, not only extended hospitality with snacks but also facilitated a favorable deal on stock, assisting us in loading our 2 wheeler.

Upon our return, we strategically identified a bustling location to set up our stall, ingeniously utilizing my sister's house without incurring any rental expense. The supportive family observed with curiosity and +anticipation as our entrepreneurial efforts unfolded, with and by 3 PM, not a single sale had materialized.

Undeterred, we persevered, driven by an unyielding determination and an unwavering belief in our venture.

Gradually, a curious crowd gathered, unexpectedly bolstered by the unexpected support of my other friends.

Within two days, more than half of our stock had been successfully sold, surprising even ourselves. Encouraged by this initial success, we regularly refilled our stock, sustaining the momentum with each passing day. Despite having utilized only half of the intended capital investment, our entrepreneurial venture flourished, firmly asserting the age-old adage that where there is a will, there is indeed away.

Conclusion & Learnings: During adolescence, the spark of entrepreneurship continued to burn brightly, despite financial limitations. Teaming up with a like-minded friend, we dreamt of launching local stores but faced capital constraints. A solution emerged during the became the seed capital. Facing challenges in sourcing, we embarked on a secret 60 km journey, relying on hospitality from strangers and strategic planning. Our makeshift stall at my sister's house started slow, but determination prevailed, and unexpected support led to success. This venture taught me that resourcefulness, determination, and unexpected support can turn constraints into opportunities.

"Business opportunities are like buses, there's always another one coming." - Richard Branson

"Corporate Crossroads: Navigating Between Career and Entrepreneurial Dreams"

The threshold of my twenties marked a poignant juncture as the stark reality of my father's impending retirement cast its shadow. His pension, unfortunately, proved to be a meager lifeline for our household, catapulting me into a realm of challenging decisions. Despite the abundance of innovative business ideas brimming within me, the weight of familial responsibilities directed me towards a more conventional path. The objective: secure a job that could shoulder the financial burden on my parents.

Thus, I found myself relocating to Hyderabad, taking the first steps in a corporate journey as a customer service representative—a humble initiation into the professional arena. This decision, greeted with joy and optimism by my parents, became a pivotal moment where I not only climbed the professional ladder but also embarked on profound personal transformations. In the midst of this transformative period, the once reserved and shy individual within me found unexpected avenues for growth and self-discovery.

The passing years witnessed the flourishing of my professional life. Scaling five rungs on the corporate ladder, I undertook a significant project transition in the USA. Simultaneously, my personal life unfolded beautifully as I entered the realm of marriage, creating an illusion of harmonious existence.

Yet, beneath this veneer of perfection, a subtle void began to manifest. A profound discontentment crept in as I grappled with the realization that I wasn't truly pursuing my desires. Despite leading a team, I lacked a sense of ownership, tethered to someone else's vision.

stories of successful startups fueled a growing admiration for these founders. In my eyes, they resembled superheroes, prompting me to immerse myself in a wealth of startup-related content, absorbing lessons and insights like a sponge.

As time elapsed, the allure of abandoning my job to embark on a new venture became irresistible. However, the practicalities of navigating middle-class constraints introduced a myriad of challenges. Consultations with numerous people, explanations of plans, establishment of understandings, and, most crucially, the daunting task of convincing others became the framework of my reality.

Consequently, I found myself leading a compromised existence, seeking solace in newfound hobbies such as cooking and traveling. However, beneath this apparent contentment, the ember of entrepreneurial dreams smoldered silently within me, waiting for the opportune moment to ignite.

entrepreneurial dreams collide, exploring the internal struggle of balancing personal aspirations with external expectations. It delves into the complexities of navigating career choices while harboring unfulfilled entrepreneurial ambitions, setting the stage for subsequent chapters where these dreams find a way to flourish.

Conclusion & Learnings: In my learnings, I faced a crucial point where family needs led me to a corporate path despite dreams of starting my own business.

Climbing the corporate ladder brought personal growth, but a hidden void emerged—I was working for someone else's vision. Drawn to entrepreneurship, challenges Within middle-class constraints led to a compromised life.

Amidst apparent contentment in hobbies like cooking and travel, the spark of entrepreneurial dreams quietly waited. This phase captures an inner struggle, paving the way for the pursuit of these dreams in the chapters ahead.

keep a good attitude while waiting." - Joyce Meyer

"Idea Genesis to Startup Reality: Navigating Challenges and Embracing Collaboration"

In the relentless pursuit of knowledge and the ever-evolving landscape of startup insights, my entrepreneurial spirit surged like an unstoppable tide. Immersed in fervent discussions with a circle of like-minded friends, I found myself gravitating towards a unique synergy. These individuals weren't just friends; they were torchbearers of technical expertise, each boasting an impressive 3 to 5 years of hands-on experience in development. It was in the crucible of these passionate exchanges that I realized the potential for a collective venture.

As the seeds of my startup dreams germinated, I instinctively turned to these friends, not merely as sources of inspiration but as the envisioned architects of my entrepreneurial journey. The decision wasn't solely driven by their technical prowess; it was a recognition of the shared vision, trust, and unwavering commitment that had organically woven our conversations into the fabric of mutual aspirations.

We explored the vast landscape of app ideas, contemplating everything from gaming apps to utility tools like speech-to-text conversion— I assume the concept we brainstormed before mainstream search engines even incorporated this feature. The genesis of this idea occurred during a drive, where the urgent need to handle important messages sparked the innovative thought process.

Another impactful concept emerged from volunteering at a blind school, a place where visually impaired children exhibited unwavering optimism in their activities.

Witnessing their unique learning process audio. The annual call for volunteers to convert textbooks to speech underscored the potential for social impact. Discussing the feasibility with developer friends, this particular concept gained traction as a potential endeavor with a profound purpose.

Amongst the myriad of ideas, the challenge was to sift through and finalize one with substantial revenue potential. After careful consideration, we settled on a concept related to visitor/security management and

apartment maintenance, naming it "aptap" (Apt App/Apartment App). While existing apps predominantly focused on gated communities with subscription models, our vision aimed at catering to standalone apartments with a freemium model, specifically targeting the dynamic demographic of middle-class millennials. Monetization strategies ranged from earning commissions on online bill payments to integrating with e-commerce, delivery, and cab vendors' APIs to garner commissions from aggregators.

Empowered by this chosen idea, I collaborated with the developer friends and gave them some time to develop a to be slower than anticipated, ultimately prompting me to make the bold decision to leave my job. Convincing my family, especially addressing prevalent gender biases, presented a formidable challenge. Fortunately, my wife supported my decision, taking charge of home affairs and finances. Recognizing the need for a calculated risk, I ventured into creating a passive income stream by operating a cab with the assistance of a third- party vendor.

However, the realization dawned that my team lacked the necessary dedication, hindering progress despite the passage of months. The passion for launching the app persisted, marking my first significant hurdle as I found myself jobless.

A pivotal moment materialized when a tech-savvy cousin expressed keen interest in joining. Together, we founded our company, Aptap, initially operating from a modest flat due to budget constraints. However, the primary challenge now shifted to hiring skilled resources with limited funds, prompting us to ponder: How can we

Conclusion & Learnings: In the pursuit of startup insights, my entrepreneurial journey ignited through passionate discussions with technically adept friends. Together, we envisioned and explored diverse app ideas, with two impactful concepts emerging – one born from a drive's inspiration and the other sparked by volunteering at a blind school. Amid challenges and slow progress, the decision to leave my job was bold but necessary.

Supported by a tech-savvy cousin, we founded Aptap, focusing on visitor/security management and apartment maintenance. Operating from a modest flat, the pivotal challenge shifted to hiring skilled resources with limited funds, marking the next crucial phase of our startup odyssey.

"If you've got an idea, start today. There's no better time than now to get going. That doesn't mean quit your job and jump into your idea 100 percent from day one, but there's always small progress that can be made to start the movement." -Kevin Systrom

"Navigating The Entrepreneurial Odyssey: Mentorship, Networking, and Unseen Allies"

Embarking on the entrepreneurial journey, I found myself in a transitional phase after leaving my job. The realization dawned about the need for guidance in this unfamiliar startup environment, especially considering my lack of a business background and familial support.

Deliberating on the ideal mentor, I reached out to a senior executive from my previous workplace, now retired and dedicated to assisting entrepreneurs. Despite not having his contact number, a social media message initiated a positive response. A phone conversation ensued, during which I candidly expressed my plans to launch an app, eagerly seeking his valuable insights.

The prospect of meeting this seasoned professional left me a bit nervous, considering his high-ranking position in my former company. Nevertheless, I knew him to be down-to-earth, and my anticipation was met with warmth as he graciously opened his office door upon my arrival.

The meeting unfolded with introductions and a deep dive into my startup idea. Lasting more than an hour, he not only appreciated the concept but also shared insightful inputs based on his wealth of experience. Emphasizing that the final decisions rested with me as the brainchild owner, he extended an offer to reach out if I encountered obstacles in my entrepreneurial journey.

Recognizing the importance of periodic mentorship meetings, I planned to reconnect after the app's launch, especially during its initial stages where guidance would prove invaluable.

As my startup journey continued evolving, I seized the opportunity to connect with another individual through a startup networking community. This individual, a successful entrepreneur running a logistics startup, graciously agreed to a meeting. By this time, my founding team had undergone changes. During our interaction, we exchanged profound insights about our respective startups, discussing unique selling points, revenue models, and operational strategies. Surprisingly, he advised considering a return to employment until our startup achieved substantial revenues, given our low ticket size.

Though I absorbed valuable inputs from these seasoned entrepreneurs, my belief in our product's potential for traction and revenue growth in the coming quarters remained unwavering.

Participating in startup communities and maintaining connections with like-minded professionals proved instrumental. Networking extended beyond industry peers, encompassing individuals from diverse roles.

valuable sounding board for ideas and challenges.

In the entrepreneurial journey, the path chosen may lead to moments of solitude or feeling overlooked. However, amidst these challenges, there are individuals who reach out, inquire about your well-being, and take the time for in-person meetings. One such person, despite relocating due to a new job, consistently scheduled meetings, attentively listened to my story, and shared valuable insights based on his extensive experience. These individuals, often considered secret mentors, quietly contribute to your growth without explicitly assuming the mentorship role, always striving to witness your success at grand scales.

Conclusion & Learnings: This chapter from my journey underscores the transformative role of mentorship, networking, and often-unseen allies in the entrepreneurial odyssey. It illuminates the profound significance of seeking guidance from experienced individuals, navigating within the vibrant startup emphasizes the dynamic interplay of mentorship, highlighting how it acts as a compass, steering

entrepreneurs through challenges. Moreover, it sheds light on the invaluable networks woven within startup ecosystems, emphasizing the collective strength derived from collaborative connections. In this exploration, the chapter unfolds the multifaceted tapestry of support that intricately shapes the entrepreneurial journey.

"A mentor is someone who allows you to see the hope inside yourself." Oprah Winfrey

"From Concept to Team: Navigating the Formation of a Startup Core"

In the embryonic stages of our entrepreneurial voyage, the foundation of our startup was laid within the confines of a friend's bachelor flat turned makeshift office. This unassuming location became the epicenter of creativity, collaboration, and the birthplace of our startup dreams.

The friend who generously provided this space emerged as more than a mere host; he became an integral part of the founding team, a collaborator in transforming raw ideas into tangible concepts.

Within this joint venture, the collaborative effort was pivotal. Together, we huddled over laptops, sketching life into our collective vision. The camaraderie within this incubation space was not just about physical proximity; it was about the synergy of minds converging to shape our startup's identity.

With the blueprint of our plan reaching its final iteration, the next critical step loomed on the horizon – finding the capable coder who could translate our vision into digital reality. Serendipity intervened when another friend, boasting over a decade of experience in technology, expressed eagerness to join our team. This seasoned addition brought not just technical prowess but a shared passion for our startup dreams. Collaborative brainstorming sessions ensued, refining the app's flow and features. The culmination of these efforts crystallized into a concrete plan, prompting us to enlist the services of a freelancing team to commence the app development process.

The development journey, though not devoid of challenges and occasional delays, witnessed unwavering commitment. We adhered to our agreement, making Simultaneously, my co-founder assumed the mantle of leading the hiring process for backend development, leveraging my prior experience in recruitment. I took charge of reviewing job description drafts meticulously crafted by the founding team members. Employing a rigorous screening process, I delved into the profiles of potential candidates, posing fundamental questions that aimed to unearth their commitment to the dynamic startup environment and assess the likelihood of long-term dedication. Those who successfully navigated this initial scrutiny were extended invitations for in-person interviews, providing an opportunity for a thorough assessment of their technical skills.

This multifaceted approach served a dual purpose – not only did it lay the bedrock for our startup's operational structure, but it also fostered the assembly of a dedicated team poised for success in the competitive business landscape. The hiring process wasn't just about skills; it was about finding individuals who shared our ethos, who believed in the journey as much as the destination.

Conclusion & Learnings: Journey from conceptualization to team formation. It unveils the collaborative efforts within the startup's birthplace, shedding light on the recruitment strategies employed. The commitment to building a team that not only possesses the requisite skills but aligns with the values and vision propelling the startup forward. Delves into the meticulous process of assembling a group of individuals who share a common purpose, emphasizing the importance of cohesive teamwork in translating ideas into actionable initiatives.

"Your work is going to fill a large part of your life, and the only way to be truly satisfied is to do what you believe is great work. And the only way to do great work is to love what you do."

–Steve Jobs

"Navigating App Development: Choosing the Right Team for Startup Success"

As we delved into the realm of mobile app development for our startup, we encountered the crucial decision of selecting the most fitting approach. Three primary avenues beckoned, each with its own merits and challenges. The first involved establishing an in-house development team, dedicated solely to our project. The second option entailed outsourcing tasks to a specialized firm with expertise in crafting apps. The third avenue beckoned us to collaborate closely with experienced freelancers, each bringing their unique skills to the table.

Initially we opted for the freelancing route. The team we engaged showcased an impressive track record, boasting meticulous organization, which included regular sprint calls, and a well-structured development model, unforeseen challenges emerged, causing disruptions in the project's progress. This prompted a reconsideration of our strategy.

While outsourcing remained a viable option, it presented challenges, particularly given our startup's constrained budget. It became clear that, irrespective of the chosen approach, having an in-house development team was indispensable for crucial tasks such as app enhancements, incorporating user feedback, and ensuring continuous development. With this realization, we decided to assemble a team of Android and iOS developers, each possessing 1 to 2 years of experience – a choice aligned with our budgetary constraints.

The hiring process involved screening numerous profiles, and when the designated day arrived, we encountered a unique challenge. Operating from a flat and receiving a significant number of applications from female candidates, we recognized the need to transition to all founding team members.

This transition not only facilitated smoother operations but also allowed for morning meetings where our tech co-founder could provide crucial directions before embarking on their daily job commitments. As the sole full-time member of the startup, I collaborated with others who balanced their roles in both employment and startup responsibilities. Eventually, we curated an in-house development team comprising skilled iOS and Android developers, backend specialists, and enthusiastic interns.

Although our initial financial capacity limited our ability to offer competitive salaries, we articulated a compelling vision – assuring prospective team members that their commitment would bear fruit as the startup gained momentum and entered a phase of exponential growth. This strategic approach ensured that our team was not only passionate about the project but also aligned with the overarching goals of the startup.

Conclusion & Learnings: The journey of navigating app development, underscoring pivotal decision of assembling the right team. Exploring the challenges encountered during the freelancing phase, providing insights into the strategic shift towards cultivating an in- house team. The unique considerations that have shaped our startup's evolving approach to app development.

Through this exploration, we learned the dynamic decision-making process, the adaptability required in a startup environment, and the strategic considerations that contribute to the development of a robust and dedicated team to drive the app development endeavors forward.

"Great things in business are never done by one person. They're done by a team of people."

- Steve Jobs

"Launching Into the Unknown: Beta Versions, Challenges, and Strategic Pivots"

This pivotal phase of our entrepreneurial journey unfolded with a palpable sense of excitement, as we found ourselves equipped with our own office space and financial resources. With funds secured for a year, our strategic plan aimed at unveiling the beta version in the first quarter. The lion's share of the investment stemmed from the co-founder and myself, while other co- founders, playing supportive roles, made minimal contributions and held modest stakes in the company.

As we welcomed new team members, the onboarding process became a knowledge-sharing endeavor. Our However, despite having three tech-oriented founders, the challenge of meeting deadlines persisted, occasionally causing delays in our development sprints.

Acknowledging the necessity for an experienced mobile app developer, our quest led us to someone with over eight years of expertise and a proven track record.

Identifying a candidate eager to collaborate with startups, we devised a flexible arrangement, allowing them to freelance as needed, working from our office two to three days a week while staying within 20% of our monthly budget.

Our progress gained momentum, achieving a frequency of at least two releases per week for Android, though iOS development remained a persistent challenge. To bridge this gap, I redirected my focus towards web and Android launches while concurrently developing the iOS version.

Exploring potential revenue streams beyond the core app functionality, we ventured into partnerships with third-home automation (IoT). However, integrating with major market aggregators presented hurdles, requiring a minimum user base before they would consider integration. In response, we strategically highlighted these upcoming features on our homepage to keep users informed.

Approaching the launch of our initial beta version, our sales and marketing efforts intensified. Presenting the app to various apartment management teams resulted in mixed responses. Some embraced the innovative free offering, while others questioned the value proposition.

Our unique revenue model involved providing free apartment activities and generating income through commissions from third-party services. Simultaneously, we tackled marketing challenges by recruiting interns who eagerly engaged in real-time projects, creating demo videos and flyers within the constraints of our tight budget.

standard apartments, feedback highlighted shortcomings for gated communities. This feedback became the cornerstone for our next steps as we strategized further improvements, honing in on enhancing features for this specific segment.

Simultaneously, faced with financial constraints, my co-founder and I implemented cost-cutting measures, a challenging yet indispensable aspect of our entrepreneurial journey.

Conclusion & Learnings: The excitement of securing office space and funds for a year, aiming to unveil the beta version strategically. While co-founders made varying contributions, team onboarding became a knowledge-sharing endeavor. Despite three tech-oriented founders, meeting deadlines remained challenging. The quest for an experienced mobile app developer led to a flexible arrangement, boosting progress. The team's

Android releases thrived, but iOS development posed persistent challenges, prompting a strategic redirection. Exploring revenue streams expanded into partnerships Faced with financial constraints, cost-cutting measures were implemented, emphasizing the indispensable nature of financial management in the entrepreneurial journey.

"The only place where success comes before work is in the dictionary."

- Vidal Sassoon

"Redesign Realities: Navigating User Feedback and Office Woes"

Receiving user feedback marked a pivotal moment in our startup journey. It revealed a common thread – users found our User Interface confusing, prompting a critical reassessment. The overwhelming number of features had unintentionally diverted attention from the core purpose of the application. In response, we embarked on a comprehensive redesign, seeking to streamline and refocus on the essential features that truly mattered to apartment living.

Understanding the user perspective became our guiding principle. Users craved an intuitive experience, desiring Our primary focus shifted to simplifying processes, ensuring tasks like making maintenance payments and logging building-related complaints could be achieved with just a few taps. Customizable society notifications were prioritized, designed to be easily accessible without interfering with users' productive time.

Despite possessing end-to-end knowledge of the product, the redesign and subsequent relaunch posed formidable challenges. The time and effort invested in this phase inevitably impacted costs, forcing us to strike a delicate balance between delivering an enhanced user experience and managing budget constraints. In the face of these challenges, our freelancing UX designer, unfortunately, became unavailable. To keep the momentum, I stepped into the role, personally contributing to the design of the screens. This hands-on involvement underscored the adaptability and exposure inherent in startup environments.

In a strategic cost-cutting move, we made the decision to vacate our office space, allowing our developers to agreed to release the advance amount, deviating from the two-month notice as per the agreement, he later balked at returning the advance amount, citing a two-month prior intimation clause in our agreement.

But After negotiations, we secured approval to vacate the office after one month, allowing the team to seamlessly transition to a remote work setup.

Conclusion & Learnings: Receiving pivotal user feedback prompted a critical reassessment of our startup journey. The revelation that our User Interface was confusing led to a comprehensive redesign, focusing on simplification and user-centricity. Understanding users' desire for an intuitive experience, we streamlined essential features to minimize navigation time. Despite challenges in the redesign phase, including the unavailability of our UX designer, hands-on involvement demonstrated adaptability. A strategic cost-cutting move involved transitioning to remote work, with negotiations resolving unforeseen challenges with the landlord. This journey underscored the importance of user-centricity,

"If you are not embarrassed by the first version of your product, you've launched too late." – Reid Hoffman, LinkedIn co-founder"

"Unexpected Turns: Lessons in App Development and Unforeseen Alliances"

The release of the beta version marked a pivotal moment as I encouraged my community members to download the app and share their thoughts. Surprisingly, less than 50% of my community engaged with the app, with only a handful offering feedback. One individual, however, meticulously examined every feature, providing a comprehensive list of insights. His valuable input became a source of joy, leading to the implementation of several of his suggestions by the team.

A few months later, this same individual expressed his interest in pursuing his ideas and sought guidance on the software development company, and finding a committed freelancer with specific deadlines. Curious about my progress, he inquired about my journey. I shared my experiences and mentioned finalizing an efficient freelancer. Intriguingly, this gentleman's cousin became the first intern at Aptap.

As time progressed, delays in app enhancements became apparent. Struggling to get a proper response from the freelancer, I persisted even while traveling to my hometown for important matters. Eventually, an update arrived, revealing that my neighbor, who had several meetings with the freelancer, was offered the CTO position with a stake in the company and a slight increase in his current package. Regrettably, he communicated that he could no longer contribute to Aptap.

In an unexpected turn of events, this gentleman approached my first intern, obtained the freelancer's contact, and arranged a series of meetings. Expressing my concerns about the impact on my app development, good to people may not always yield positive outcomes.

This incident became another lesson - the path of kindness may not always be reciprocated in a beneficial manner. Despite setbacks, he went on to build a successful delivery app in a Tier III city during the challenging times of COVID, expanding to multiple locations, and thriving in his business today.

Conclusion & Learnings: The beta version release marked a pivotal moment, evoking limited community engagement. However, a meticulous individual's comprehensive feedback became a source of joy, leading to valuable improvements. When he expressed interest in app development, I shared insights. Intriguingly, his cousin became Aptap's first intern. Delays in enhancements arose, and the freelancer's departure, offering the CTO position to my neighbor, posed challenges. Despite concerns, my neighbor's subsequent success with a delivery app highlighted the unpredictability of outcomes. This journey emphasized the significance of resilience, adaptability, and the entrepreneurship.

"In the midst of challenges, there are hidden opportunities, and in the face of unpredictability, resilience becomes the compass guiding us through the dynamic journey of entrepreneurship."

-Unknown

"Navigating Challenges: The Rise and Fall of My Startup Journey"

In our relentless pursuit of cost-cutting measures, despite exploring every conceivable avenue, we found ourselves inevitably grappling with a financial shortfall. The stark disparity between working in a traditional office setting and transitioning to remote work took its toll, causing a noticeable dip in overall productivity.

As we lagged two months behind in salary payments, the resilient team persevered with unwavering determination. My co-founder remained steadfast in his pursuit of securing additional funding, emphasizing that we were on the brink of success. However, in light of the approach. I've explained few reasons on my fundingperception in next chapter.

Opting to relaunch the project with the resources at our disposal seemed like a prudent decision, allowing us to assess our needs moving forward.

Just as we were navigating these challenges, news of the impending COVID-19 pandemic began to surface.

Recognizing the profound impact it would have on the fabric of human existence, we accelerated our development efforts, anticipating a surge in digital payments. However, our hopes were dashed when the lockdown was enforced earlier than anticipated.

Faced with an insoluble dilemma, the only recourse was to shut down operations and release the team to move on. It was a moment of helplessness, with no one to hold accountable except myself. Just before the lockdown was imposed, a personal obligation necessitated my visit to my hometown, inadvertently leading to a three-month solace in the safety of togetherness. Despite the challenging circumstances, my mother's worry-free demeanor brought a semblance of happiness to our temporary refuge.

The mantra "Stay home – Stay safe" became the new norm, and we embraced it wholeheartedly. Our days were filled with culinary adventures, board games, and binge-watching on OTT platforms. Simultaneously, my team members had dispersed to their respective hometowns, and I maintained constant communication, keeping tabs on their well-being.

In a heartening turn of events, my sister's family initiated a noble cause, extending assistance to underprivileged individuals within their community. Providing essential supplies such as groceries, vegetables, medicines, sanitizers, and masks, they focused on supporting those dependent on daily wages, including plumbers, carpenters, painters, and electricians. The shared

experiences of individuals facing challenging times and unemployment have left a lasting impact on my importance of empathy, support, and collective efforts to address such issues. The narratives of resilience in the face of adversity inspire a deeper understanding of the human experience and fuel a commitment to contributing positively to the well-being of others.

The broader impact of the COVID-19 pandemic was undeniably devastating, with families grappling with profound losses. As lockdown restrictions gradually eased, a semblance of normalcy returned, albeit with the imperative of maintaining safe distances.

Yet, amidst these external developments, my mind remained entrenched in the aftermath of my startup's demise. Acceptance proved to be an elusive concept, a lingering struggle against the harsh reality.

Conclusion & Learnings: In our pursuit of cost-cutting measures, a financial shortfall emerged, exacerbated by the productivity dip in transitioning to remote work.

Lagging in salary payments, the resilient team imminent COVID-19 pandemic accelerated development efforts, but the lockdown thwarted our plans. Faced with an unsolvable dilemma, shutting down operations became inevitable. A personal obligation led to an unexpected three-month lockdown confinement in my hometown, bringing solace in family togetherness.

Despite challenges, we embraced the "Stay home – Stay safe" mantra, finding solace in shared experiences and initiating a noble cause to support the underprivileged amid the broader impact of the pandemic. Acceptance of the startup's demise remained elusive, a lingering struggle against harsh reality.

"I knew that if I failed I wouldn't regret that, but I knew the one thing I might regret is not trying."

– Jeff Bezos

"Equity and Pressure- The Dual Faces of Startup Financing"

Your choice to refrain from fundraising is rooted in a comprehensive understanding of the challenges and implications associated with external capital. The intricacies of equity dilution, involving a deliberate relinquishment of a percentage of your company in exchange for capital, extend beyond immediate financial gain.

This process not only entails sharing future profits but also necessitates surrendering a portion of decision- making power to investors, thus reshaping power dynamics within the business. The perpetual pressure to perform post-funding, driven by investor expectations

The prospect of a loss of control, inherent in entrusting a part of your startup to external investors, demands astute management to balance investor expectations with the core values and goals intrinsic to your vision. The time- consuming nature of the fundraising process, involving crafting compelling pitches, engaging with potential investors, and negotiating terms, diverts attention from day-to-day operations, prompting a strategic approach to mitigate potential disruptions.

Furthermore, the additional hurdles of interest and repayment in debt financing are acknowledged, particularly if the path to profitability extends beyond the initial projections. While acknowledging the undeniable benefits of startup funding for accelerated growth, your deliberate consideration of these multifaceted factors aligned with your unique business goals and values underscores a prudent decision-making approach. The emphasis on seeking investors whose vision aligns with your startup's long-term trajectory reflects a commitment to fostering a harmonious and mutually beneficial partnership.

Conclusion & Learnings: Embarking on external funding involves crucial considerations. Equity dilution demands sharing profits and decision-making power, altering power dynamics. The pressure to perform arises with investor expectations for fruitful returns, potentially conflicting with long-term visions. The loss of control is inherent, as external investors may diverge from your startup's core values. Fundraising proves time-consuming, diverting focus from day-to-day operations.

Debt financing introduces interest and repayment challenges. While funding accelerates growth, careful consideration of these factors, aligned with business goals, is vital. Choosing investors aligned with your startup's long-term trajectory fosters a more harmoniousand mutually beneficial partnership.

"In the journey of entrepreneurship, external funding is a compass, guiding through the terrain of challenges, where every decision shapes the landscape of success."

- Unknown

"The Journey of 'QuikServ' and the Rise of a Purposeful Second Venture"

Despite certain lockdown exceptions, the ability to travel was still constrained. During my strolls, I encountered numerous faces marked by sadness and hunger, a reflection of the limited employment opportunities available, especially for those dependent on daily wages.

Motivated by a desire to assist these vulnerable workers, I compiled a list of individuals who had shared their stories of unemployment with us. This prompted the inception of "QuikServ," a social media platform dedicated to home repairs and maintenance services. The range of services offered, including home sanitization, plumbing, carpentry, house painting, and electrical work, attracted attention.

To kickstart the initiative, I shared the social media pages within my network, leading to an unexpected surge in service requests. The demand for home and commercial disinfection and sanitization services particularly stood out, garnering a significant response.

As word of our endeavor spread, vendors expressed interest in joining our platform, expanding our service offerings to thirteen categories. Managing orders, payments, and vendor relationships became my responsibility, necessitating a cash-based payment system for most vendors. Recognizing the importance of adhering to COVID norms, I provided behavioral skills training to vendors and emphasized maintaining social distance during service delivery.

Recognizing the potential for growth, I decided to transform this venture into my second startup. Drawing from the lessons of my first startup, I opted not to invest until a stable revenue stream was established. To ensure fairness, I communicated to vendors that a commission would be charged only on orders surpassing a certain threshold, not on minimum transactions.

Launching this business during a time when homes had been neglected for months due to lockdown proved opportune. Within a couple of months, revenues soared into six digits, marking steady growth month after month.

As lockdown restrictions eased, I returned to Hyderabad, overseeing operations remotely. The idea of expansion took root, leading me to gather contacts in new cities and explore the potential for growth. While some orders thrived, a few encountered setbacks due to vendors failing to fulfill commitments. Expansion to outside customers was momentarily paused, but services continued within my friends' circle.

Eager to explore untapped markets, I considered tier III cities where market leaders were yet to establish a foothold. Leveraging my network, I enlisted passionate individuals in seven tier III cities to form teams and align vendors. The plan included launching an app and subsequently introducing services in these cities.

However, an unforeseen second wave of the pandemic dampened our progress. People became reluctant to allow outsiders into their homes, leading to a decline in service orders. The challenging period compelled us to wait patiently for a return to normalcy.

During this time, some former employees from my first startup successfully launched delivery apps in their own towns. Their success was attributed to a combination of passion for entrepreneurship, optimal timing, and a lack of competition in tier III cities. Inspired by their achievements, I mentored one of these startups as they expanded into service-based offerings.

Continuing my commitment to fostering entrepreneurship, I offer guidance to aspiring entrepreneurs in planning and execution, ensuring that their endeavors are equipped for success.

Conclusion & Learnings: In the wake of restricted travel during the lockdown, witnessing faces marked by sadness and hunger inspired the creation of "QuikServ," a platform offering home repair and maintenance services. The venture, kickstarted through social media, experienced an unexpected surge in demand, particularly for disinfection services. Scaling up, vendors joined, expanding services to thirteen categories. Transforming it into my second startup, I learned from the first venture, ensuring a stable revenue stream before investment. As revenues soared into six digits within months, expansion plans took root. The second pandemic wave posed challenges, requiring patience, and former employees' successful startups inspired mentorship in entrepreneurship, fostering growth and success.

"Expect change. Analyze the landscape. Take the opportunities. Stop being the chess piece; become the player. It's your move."

-Tony Robbins

www.ingramcontent.com/pod-product-compliance
Lightning Source LLC
LaVergne TN
LVHW041540070526
838199LV00046B/1752